Forward

This guide is written with the assumption that the player is not playing the tutorial missions. This guide's goal is to provide insight on how to handle the various aspects of the game, XCOM 2, with all DLC installed. The player has many choices to make in XCOM 2 which this guide will hopefully simplify. Bear in mind that there are many possible approaches to the game but this guide is going to be guided by how I approach the game.

Scott O'Brady - More than 10,000 hours recorded on Steam playing XCOM 2

The First Screens

Several screens can be accessed from the first screen that appears in XCOM 2. New games can be started and saves can be reloaded. Multiplayer mode, challenge mode and the legacy hub do not allow the use of mods and will not be covered in any detail.

The options button allows access to hardware settings, frequency settings for soldier customization which applies to randomly created characters, and the character pool where characters can be edited, created, deleted, imported or exported. Character backstories, appearance, nationality and how they can appear, soldier, VIP or enemy VIP, can all be edited.

On the character pool screen at the bottom is button to choose between character pool only, random only or character pool and random. Unless a large character pool has been developed random characters should also be allowed.

The new game button will start the process for creating a new campaign. There are several choices that can be made before the new campaign starts.

Beta strike - Increases the hit points of units which makes tactical engagements longer. This makes the game more difficult especially if using some of the modded enemies that are available.

Reaper ally - Start the game with a reaper in your roster. This makes the early part of the game easier due to the excellent stealth ability of the reaper.

Skirmisher ally - Start the game with a skirmisher in your roster. The skirmisher is a very strong soldier in the early game due to multiple shots and high mobility.

Templar ally - Start the game with a templar in your roster. The templar's excellent melee ability helps a lot in the early game, especially against sectoids due to the vulnerability of sectoids to melee attack. The templar's ability to strike and get out of trouble is also very useful.

Grim horizon - Dark events are permanent. This definitely makes the game more difficult, especially if some of the terrible dark events appear very early in the game.

Lengthy scheme - Doubles the length of the Avatar project. This makes the strategic part of the game much easier. There will not be as much pressure to locate enemy facilities for assault or expand to new areas in the game.

Time turner - Doubles the length of mission timers. This makes the missions with timers a lot easier simplifying the tactical game.

Precision explosives - Grenade damage falls off from the center which makes the tactical game harder.

On the next screen seen when creating a new campaign players choose between iron man mode and regular mode. If using many mods or ones that make dramatic changes to the game it is best to not choose iron man mode since mods can sometimes lead to crashes which only can be discovered with extensive play testing.

After the iron man screen comes the optional narrative content screen. If the Lost and Abandoned mission is chosen then the first chosen encountered will be the assassin. If not chosen the first could be any of the three. The Lost and Abandoned mission will also result in Mox being captured and the generation of a mission to save him.

Below there are two more options, Alien Hunters "The Nest", a mission where Bradford is leading a squad on the mission and must survive. No rulers will appear until this mission has been completed if this option is chosen which makes the game easier since the player can prepare forces better to face the rulers.

If integrated, the rulers will appear at Avatar project facilities which is easier since the first engagement is determined by the player.

Allowing rulers to appear entirely at random is the toughest way to play.

The last option is for the Shen's Last Gift "Lost Towers" mission which introduces a new unit, the Spark, to the game. If this option is not chosen then research will be available to open up the Spark unit for use. Spark units can be very useful for shredding armor which becomes more important as the game progresses.

Once all these choices have been made the Gatecrasher mission begins with a starting squad of four soldiers.

The Grenadier Class

The grenadier class is deals high damage and is excellent for destroying cover, probably its most important ability. As the grenadier's equipment is improved the damage is increased as is the area of effect, both very important in the later game.The grenadier starts with the **launch grenade** ability. Grenadiers are strongest in the early part of a campaign.

At corporal the choice is between **blast padding** which increases armor by one and reduces damage from explosions by sixty-six percent and **shredder,** which becomes more and more important as the campaign progresses. The clear choice here is shredder.

At sergeant the decision is between **demolition,** which attempts to destroy cover but does no damage and **suppression,** which imposes a fifty percent penalty on attacks. The clear choice here is suppression.

As lieutenant the choice is between **heavy ordinance** which adds one more use to grenade slots and **holotargeting** which adds fifteen aim to attacks made by soldiers after the attack of the grenadier, hit or miss. Both of these abilities are very good; getting the second one in the training center is a good option.

At captain the decision is between **volatile mix,** which adds two to grenade damage and **chain shot,** which allows two shots with a fifteen percent aim penalty. Volatile mix is a little better since the damage is guaranteed.

At major the choice is between **salvo** which makes launching a grenade on the first action not cost an action and **hail of bullets** which guarantees a hit with the primary weapon. Since grenades are limited the better choice here is hail of bullets, which is also great for finishing off enemies.

At colonel the decision is between **saturation fire**, which fires a hail of bullets in an arc that damages all enemies and cover and **rupture,** which does critical damage and adds three damage to all additional sources. Rupture is the best choice for dealing with late game enemies so it is the better choice here.

The Psionic Class

The psionic class is different from all other classes in the game. Psionics don't gain rank by experience; they gain it by training in the psionics lab. Psionic abilities are listed below and the best abilities are in italics.

Soul fire - Does guaranteed damage to a target and has a three turn cool down. This ability is excellent for finishing off units.

Stasis - Stuns a target for one turn and has a three turn cool down. The target will be immune to attack. This ability is great for countering a very dangerous enemy unit or protecting a very vulnerable friendly unit if the psionic has the stasis shield ability. Stasis used on a mind controlled soldier removes the mind control and casting it on the enemy also removes it.

Insanity - A telepathic attack that can inflict negative conditions on the target that has a three turn cooldown.

Inspire - Grants a nearby friendly unit an additional action.

Soul Steal - Soul fire now heals the psionic for half the damage dealt.

Stasis Shield - Allows stasis to be cast on friendly units.

Solace - Blocks or extinguishes mental impairments on the psionic with the ability and allies within a four tile radius. Passive ability.

Sustain - If reduced to zero hit points the psionic goes into stasis with one hit point instead. Limited to once per mission. This is an ability that might be worth picking up before the final mission.

Schism - Insanity does a small amount of damage and applies rupture

to a target. This makes insanity effective at finishing off enemy
units.

Fortress - Makes the psionic immune to fire, poison, acid and
explosive damage.

Fuse - Causes enemy explosives to explode. This is great for
removing enemy cover and also saves on grenades.

Domination - Gives permanent control over an enemy unit. Only one
successful domination is allowed per mission. A failed domination
attempt results in a four turn cooldown. The stronger the psionic
the better this ability is.

Null Lance - A beam of psionic energy that damages an enemy unit.
This beam can be shot through obstacles at enemy units the psionic
can not see if another friendly unit can see the target.

Void Rift - An area of effect attack that does damage and also has a
chance to apply insanity on targets in the storm. Like null lance
this can be cast on areas the psionic can not see if seen by another
friendly unit. The explosion that results is also good for
destroying cover.

The Ranger Class

The ranger specializes in recon and close combat. The ranger starts out with **slash,** which allows the ranger to attack any enemy unit in range with a sword.

At corporal the decision is between **phantom** and **blade master**. At this point it must be decided what the dominant role for the ranger will be until the other ability can be obtained in the training center. Some rangers focused on stealth will be needed since the reaper can not provide recon on every mission. For players with a style of play that focuses less on stealth blade master is the clear choice.

At sergeant the choice is between **shadow strike** which adds aim and critical hit bonuses when attacking from stealth and **shadow step** which makes the soldier immune to overwatch. Shadow step is the clear choice since it can occur without limit and works very well with the ranger's melee ability.

At lieutenant the choice is between **conceal,** good for stealth based rangers and **run and gun,** an ability that helps the ranger get flanking attacks against enemies. Stealth based rangers should pick up run and gun in the training center.

At captain the choice is between **implacable,** which grants a bonus move after a kill, and bladestorm. Bladestorm is the best ranger ability and is very effective at ambushing enemy reinforcements but bear in mind that some units, like purifiers, explode when killed. Implacable is a worthwhile acquisition in the training center.

At major the decision rests between **deep cover** which allows rangers to hunker down if they did not attack during the turn and **untouchable** which makes the ranger immune to the next enemy attack after a kill. Untouchable is the choice here as it fits in well with the ranger's other aggressive abilities.

At colonel the choice is between **rapid fire** and **reaper**. Rapid fire is very good at damaging enemies with many hit points and reaper is very good at finishing off damaged units. This is a difficult choice but rapid fire is probably the easiest skill to use in the later part of the game when rangers can get these abilities.

The Reaper Class

The reaper is the best recon unit in the game and has the capability to do a lot of damage. The reaper starts with **shadow** which allows the reaper to stay hidden at mission start and gives a reduced chance of detection after aggressive action, which increases after subsequent actions until eventually revealed. The reaper can go back into shadow once per mission. Shadow has a reduced detection radius and increases the mobility of the reaper by fifty percent.

The second starting ability is the **claymore** which has limited uses but can become more powerful as the campaign progresses. As a hero class the reaper can gain more than one ability upon promotion even before the training center has been built.

At corporal the reaper has access to **remote start** and **blood trail**. Remote start allows the reaper to trigger environmental explosives doubling the damage and the radius. It is a much more significant increase in the reaper's ability to do damage than blood trail making it the better choice.

At sergeant the reaper has access to **target definition** which makes any enemy units seen by the reaper remain visible and **shrapnel** which adds three to claymore damage and increases the radius of the claymore by one. The reaper's greatest strength is the ability to recon for XCOM squads so the best choice here is target definition which is not limited like the claymore.

At lieutenant the reaper has access to **silent killer,** which allows the reaper to remain concealed after a vector rifle kill, **distraction,** which puts the reaper back in shadow after a claymore kill, and **needle** which adds two armor piercing to shots taken in shadow. The best of these is silent killer, which is less limited than the other two abilities.

At captain the reaper gains access to **sting**, a one-time shot that does not break concealment, and **soul harvest** which increases critical chances by five after a kill up to a maximum increase of twenty. The limitations of sting make soul harvest a better choice.

At major the reaper gains access to **highlands,** which provides the reaper with an additional claymore, and **banish,** which allows the reaper to fire repeatedly at a target until it is killed or the reaper runs out of ammunition. Banish when combined with some weapon attachments is a very strong ability and the better choice here despite the fact it breaks concealment.

At colonel the reaper has the choice between **homing mine,** which allows the reaper to attach a claymore to a target without breaking concealment, and **annihilate,** which extends the banish ability by allowing the reaper to shoot at other targets after the first is killed until all targets are dead or the reaper runs out of ammunition. It is the best choice here and very good when dealing with Avatars in the late game if the best repeaters and magazines are attached to the vektor rifle.

The Sharpshooter Class

The sharpshooter, a class that becomes more powerful compared to other classes as campaigns progress, has two main tracks, the sniper and the gunslinger which focuses on pistol skills. The sharpshooter's starting skill **squadsight** is what makes the sharpshooter a sharpshooter. Squadsight allows the sharpshooter to see any target in line of sight as long as another unit can see the target.

At corporal the choice is between **long watch**, which allows the use of squadsight on overwatch, and **return fire**, which allows firing back at an enemy once per turn. Long watch is better because it is less situational and the sharpshooter in a sniper role is seldom going to get shot at by the enemy.

At sergeant the choice is between **deadeye**, which increases damage at a small cost to aim, and **lightning hands**. which allows shooting the pistol at no cost of an action but has a three turn cool down. This is a difficult choice and depends a lot on style of play.

At lieutenant the choice is between **death from above**, which gives an additional action if an enemy is killed at a lower elevation, and **quick draw**, which allows firing the pistol on the first action without ending the turn. A sharpshooter will often be at a higher elevation and the sniper rifle does more damage so death from above is the choice at this rank.

At captain the choice is between **killzone**, which allows reaction shots against the enemy in a cone of fire, and **faceoff**, which allows a pistol shot at every available enemy. Faceoff is very useful on missions with many enemies like the lost and has more predictable results than killzone.

At major the choice is between **steady hands**, which improves aim and critical hit chance if the sharpshooter has not moved and **aim** which increases aim by twenty for the first shot after hunker down. The sharpshooter often stays in place for long periods so the best choice here is steady hands which can improve aim and critical hit chance every turn.

At colonel the choice is between **serial**, which restores actions

after kills but reduces critical hit chance on consecutive shots and
fanfire which allows three shots with a pistol at the same target.
Both of these can be very good but serial is better overall because
multiple targets can be killed in one turn. Fanfire should be
picked up in the training center.

The Skirmisher Class

    The skirmisher class is designed around the ideas of mobility and attacking multiple times. The bullpup and ripjack are the weapons of the skirmishers. The skirmishers start with the **marauder** ability, which allows the skirmisher two move or shoot actions in any order, **justice**, which is a strike with the ripjack, and **grapple**, a free action which allows quick movement to an elevated position. Skirmishers benefit most from expanded magazines, hair triggers, repeaters and autoloaders which compliment the multiple fire capability of skirmishers.

    At corporal the skirmisher gains access to **reflex**, which grants an extra action once in a mission after being fired upon, and **total combat**, which allows throwing a grenade on the first action to not end the turn. The best choice here is total combat.

    At sergeant the choice is between **wrath**, which draws the skirmisher to a target for a melee attack, and **zero in**, which increases critical hit chances by ten percent on subsequent shots in a turn and increases aim by ten percent if attacks are against the same target. Zero in is the more reliable ability here since wrath might easily expose other pods making the skirmisher vulnerable to attack.

    At lieutenant the choice is between **whiplash**, a free attack with an electric lash, and **full throttle**, which increases mobility by two for every kill in a turn. The whiplash is limited to one use so full throttle is a bit better here. Full throttle is very good in areas with the lost where kills are very easy to get.

    At captain the choice is between **combat presence**, which grants an action to a nearby ally, **retribution**, which grants a free attack like bladestorm against enemies in melee range, and **interrupt**, which allows a skirmisher to perform any action during an overwatch. Choosing between retribution and combat presence is difficult. In areas with lost retribution is the clear favorite but since combat presence has no cooldown it is also an excellent choice. Picking up the second one in the training center is a good option.

At major the choice is between **waylay,** which allows a skirmisher to take as many shots on overwatch as the skirmisher has remaining actions, and **reckoning,** which opens up a ripjack attack with a five turn cooldown. Waylay is very situational and reckoning has a very long cooldown so the choice is difficult here.

At colonel the skirmisher has the choice between **manual override,** which lowers all cooldowns by one, **battlelord,** which gives the skirmisher an action after every enemy action in line of sight, and **judgement,** which makes enemy units that attack the skirmisher check for panic after an attack. Manual override is very good if many abilities with cooldowns have been chosen. battlelord is very situational but in a place with many enemies like places with the lost it can be very good. Judgement has no cooldown and is a passive ability making it a good pick. The best pick depends on what abilities the skirmisher has and how the skirmisher is used in a campaign.

The Specialist Class

The specialist armed with the gremlin provides support for XCOM units. The specialist has two main tracks, battle medic and combat hacker. The class starts out with **hack** and **aid**, which provides additional defense to a unit. These abilities can be done remotely using the gremlin.

At corporal the choice is the most difficult between **medical protocol**, which allows the gremlin to heal soldiers at range, and **combat protocol**, which allows the gremlin to damage enemy units with a jolt that can be used twice per mission. Combat protocol is excellent for finishing off damaged enemy units. The medical protocol gives medical kits an additional charge. It is worthwhile to pick up the other ability in the training center.

At sergeant the choice is between **revival protocol**, which can remove any mental effects, and **haywire protocol**, which allows the hacking of enemy units. At low rank revival may be the better choice but at higher levels with higher hacking ability haywire becomes very useful. This is another case where getting the second ability in the training center is a good option.

At lieutenant the decision is between **field medic**, which gives medical kits two additional charges, and **scanning protocol**. As the game progresses field medic becomes very useful as area weapons become more common in Advent forces. Scanners can be used by any unit so it is best to take the field medic ability, which is exclusively available to specialists.

At captain the choice is between **covering fire**, which applies overwatch to enemy actions and movement. The other option is **threat** assessment, which grants an overwatch shot to a unit when the aid protocol is used. Enemy units will often be in cover which makes defensive fire less effective so the choice here is threat assessment.

At major the decision is between **ever vigilant,** which grants overwatch after movement that takes two actions, and **guardian,** which gives a fifty percent chance of an additional overwatch shot as long as a unit has ammunition. The clear choice here is guardian which gives more shots.

At colonel the choice is between **restoration** which heals or revives every soldier as needed and capacitor **discharge** which damages and potentially stuns enemy units. Capacitor discharge does additional damage against robotic units. The drawback of capacitor discharge is that it can only be used once per mission. Restoration although also limited to one use has great potential for the final mission where it is likely units are going to be injured.

The Templar Class

    The templar is a melee class supported with psionic abilities. The templar starts with the abilities **rend**, the melee ability of the templar, **volt**, a psionic attack that costs one focus that is good for finishing off enemy units, and **focus** which allows the templar to become increasingly effective during combat.

    At corporal the templar gains access to **parry**, an essential ability for the templar that is often in the thick of battle, **aftershock**, which makes enemies struck by volt easier to hit by fifteen percent, and **amplify**, which marks a target that will take an additional 33 percent damage on single target attacks that costs one focus. Parry is the choice here but aftershock should be obtained from the training facility if feasible. Advent units will prioritize targeting templars that use the parry ability even when it is a disadvantage to do so.

    At sergeant the templar gains access to **overcharge**, which gives rend attacks a 33 percent chance to create focus, **pillar**, which creates a cover point that costs one focus, and **stun strike** which pushes an enemy unit back and costs one focus. Of these overcharge is best since so many abilities are improved by or tied to focus.

    At lieutenant the templar gains access to **deflect**, which gives the templar a chance to deflect shots and if the templar has focus and **channel**, which gives a chance that enemy units that die may leave behind focus. Deflect supports the templar melee abilities nicely and is a good choice here. Abilities that generate focus, like channel, are also good.

    At captain the templar gains access to **reflect**, which requires deflect and two focus. Reflect gives the templar a chance to direct incoming shots back at the attacker. **Invert** allows the templar to switch positions with an enemy unit. This is a very good ability to have when encountering the Chosen in their lairs. **Deep focus** increases the possible focus level to three. These make for a tough choice but if facing enemies that move after being hit which can sometimes be a quality of the Chosen and is a quality of Avatars then invert is a good choice. Deep focus is also good since so many abilities depend on focus.

At major the templar gains access to **arc wave**, which improves the rend attack, and **exchange**, which allows the templar to switch places with a squad mate. Since melee is the dominant templar ability arc wave is the choice here.

At colonel the templar gains access to **ionic storm**, which strikes all nearby enemies but costs all focus, **void conduit**, which traps a humanoid unit for multiple actions and transfers health to the templar. The last ability obtained is **ghost**, which creates a duplicate of the body from a fallen humanoid. Ghosts can not regain focus which makes them weak but this can be changed using the mod, A Better Ghost. Void conduit is the easiest of these skills to use.

The Spark Class

The Spark is the MEC unit for XCOM; it is designed to be able to take and dish out damage. The spark is very good at shredding armor. The spark also can handle many of the hacking duties just like a specialist. There are two drawbacks to spark units in the standard game. They could be quite weak if encountered late in a game, and they can be expensive which makes other classes a better investment because upgrades apply to many and not to a few. Sparks do not benefit from cover but can hide behind it.

The spark starts with **overdrive** which is a very powerful skill that gives three actions. Shots after the first will have a penalty applied which can be removed with a later spark skill. The sparks weapon has built in shredding ability. It is immune to fire and poison which is very good when dealing with chryssalids. The last starting ability is hack which allows the spark to take the place of a specialist.

At the second rank, aspirant, the spark has the choice between **bulwark** which increases armor by one and allows the spark to provide high cover for adjacent friendly units, and **adaptive aim**, which removes the penalties on multiple shots. Adaptive aim is the choice here. The bulwark ability also provides cover to Advent units next to the spark.

At the third rank, knight, the spark unit has access to rainmaker, which improves the damage to heavy weapons by two and increases the radius of AOE heavy weapons by two. The alternative is **strike** which works like the slash ability of the ranger.

At the fourth rank, cavalier, the spark chooses between **intimidate**, which forces soldiers that attack the spark to save against panic, and **wrecking ball**, which allows the destruction of walls and cover.

At the fifth rank, vanguard, the spark must choose between **repair** and **bombard**. Both of these abilities have limited uses so choosing is difficult. Repair makes the spark quite strong.

At sixth rank, paladin, the spark has the choice of **channeling field**, which allows the MEC to channel energy into its heavy weapon, and **hunter protocol**, which gives the spark a 33 percent chance to take a free overwatch when an enemy is revealed. Free shots are always a good option so hunter protocol is the best choice here.

The final rank, champion, provides a choice between **sacrifice**, which directs enemy attacks against other units towards the MEC, and **nova**, which is an AOE attack that does damage to enemy forces around the MEC but temporarily stuns the spark.

More on Soldiers

Soldiers gain experience by going on missions, the greater proportion of experience points, and making kills. Soldiers only gain one promotion after a mission even if they have enough experience for two. The additional promotion will require an additional kill by the soldier. Soldiers require more experience points to level up at higher difficulty levels.

Tired soldiers are more susceptible to mental conditions like panic and mind control. Keeping a large roster of soldiers greatly reduces the need to ever take a tired soldier on a mission which could result in a negative trait which require the infirmary to remove.

There are two ways to level up rookies, training in the guerrilla tactics school and going on covert actions.

All soldier statistics improve with promotion but there is a mod, soldier development which ties the improvement of soldier statistics to what they do in combat.

The gear of soldiers left behind on a mission is lost.

Strategic Play

Base Management

In the early game there are two important considerations, making more spaces available for facilities, and building the most needed facilities early. Unless there is a compelling need for a facility early in the game a good strategy is to keep engineers focused on clearing out more spaces. Also note where the two spaces best for power relays are located and clear out debris to get to at least one of them as soon as possible. The second one is a good place for the psionics lab or the shadow chamber, facilities that require a lot of power. If a place of interest appears on the global map offering power take it; it will allow the building an additional facility before needing a power relay. Engineers are also very essential early on so pick them up at every opportunity early in the game. Only nine engineers are need to run all facilities at full capacity.

A good choice for the first facility is the resistance ring which opens up covert operations. The second choice should be the guerrilla tactics school which is needed to increase squad size. If built early in the game there is no need to speed the construction of the guerrilla tactics school since it takes some time to reach the rank required with at least one soldier to open up the first squad size upgrade.

The third choice could vary but a good option is to complete the Advent officer autopsy to open up the proving ground which is needed for a lot of the best equipment in the game. Another option is to go for resistance communications, two are needed to enable contacting all regions. The choice here depends a lot on style of play. There is no need to panic over the Avatar Project which can be controlled by covert actions and destruction of facilities. After the third facility look for the best place for a power relay.

After the first facilities are in place the next facilities are going to depend on how things are going in the game. If many soldiers are wounded or have negative traits then the infirmary is probably the right choice. If things are going very well then the psionics lab may be the choice, especially if the power is available. Another option is the shadow chamber if the research for it has been done. It provides more information on missions which is very helpful as the game progresses.

The defense matrix should be built, if possible, soon enough to aid in the Avenger defense missions. The Avenger defenses with the Chosen can be very difficult without the defense matrix. The guns often destroy cover which conserves grenades.

The workshop can be built if short engineers and there is a good spot to place the facility. The laboratory can be built if a boost in research is desired but the facility can be expensive. Once there are several soldiers with enough ability points the training facility can be built to improve existing soldier bonds and add more abilities to soldiers. There is no hurry to build any of these facilities.

Facilities do have maintenance costs that eat into supplies

available but this can be offset by doing supply raids when
available or covert actions that provide supplies as a reward.

Points of Interest

         Points of interest are points on the strategic map that need to
be scanned to get benefits.

1. **Rookies** - Important to scan in the early game when the pool of
soldiers is very small. Rookies are better than soldiers early in
the campaign because multiple rookies are obtained after a scan
instead of just one soldier of low rank.

2, **Soldier** - A good choice when the force pool of soldiers is small
but since it only results in one soldier it is not as good as a scan
as rookies.

3. **Alloys** - Scan any time alloys are low and nothing better is
available.

4. **Elerium** - Scan any time elerium is low and nothing better is
available.

5. **Alloys and Elerium** - Better than alloys or elerium because both
resources are provided when the scan is complete.

6. **Facility Lead** - Always scan these because destroying facilities
is one way to keep the Avatar Project under control. It can make
facilities in areas where XCOM is not active available for
destruction.

7. **Supply Raid** - Always a good choice since raids can provide all
resources as well as corpses.

8. **Guerrilla Op** - Results in a timed guerrilla operation which can
be a good choice if a horrible dark event is in the works. Unless the
reward is something really needed there are often better choices.

9. **Scientist** - Always a good choice in the early game. In the
later stages of the game there are rewards that can compete equally
with scientists.

10. **Engineer** - Always a good choice in the early game. In the later
game additional engineers are often no longer needed since only nine
are needed to maximize the performance of facilities.

Research

        Research is a key component of the strategic part of the game
in XCOM 2. Some technologies are more important than others.
Weapons take the greatest priority followed by armor but at some
point it is important to research resistance communications as it is
needed to expand to new areas and to get the muton autopsy out of
the way for plasma grenades.
        Breakthroughs and inspirations can occur at any time. Any that
occur for key technologies, italicized, should always be taken to
advance the main technological path.

Standard Research Projects

Alien Biotech - A viable first choice since it leads to the Advent
officer autopsy which opens up the proving ground. This research is
one of the technologies required to enable the use of PCS chips.

Alien Encryption - Opens up the option to build the shadow chamber.

Resistance Communications - Opens up the option to build the
resistance communications facility.

Resistance Radio - Allows XCOM to build radio towers to extend the
range of communications at lower intelligenceligence cost. This
technology
greatly enhances the ability to expand.

Psionics - Allows construction of the psonics lab and makes the
psionic class available for XCOM. The facility requires a lot of
energy so it can be delayed until a suitable place is available or
the needed energy is on hand.

Hybrid Materials - One of the first choices. It starts the path for
improved armor and makes the nanoscale vest available.

Plated Armor - The next main armor available and a big step up in
protection for XCOM soldiers. Get it after magnetic weapons unless
it shows up as an inspiration or a breakthrough.

Modular Weapons - Makes weapon attachments available for use. If no
weapon attachments have been obtained in the first mission then Alien
Biotech is the best choice for the first technological research. If
weapon attachments are obtained then this is a good first choice.
This is one of the required technologies for the use of PCS chips.

Magnetic Weapons - The first upgrade of XCOM weapons and should be
obtained early. It is possible to play with magnetic weapons for
quite a while until plasma becomes available.

Gauss Weapons - Makes upgrade to the cannon, sniper rifle and the

reaper's weapon available. Snipers provide excellent long range fire
so get this upgrade as soon as possible. The cannon also adds
significant punch.

Elerium - This technology opens up upgrades to power relays and is a
stepping stone on the road to plasma weapons.

Powered Armor - A nice jump in defensive and offensive power for XCOM
since it opens up the war suit and wraith suit for production in the
proving ground. The war suit adds a heavy weapon to the suit of
armor. The wraith suit is very nice for a sniper with the increased
mobility or for a soldier trying to get into an Advent facility by
the fastest route though walls.

Plasma Rifle - The first group of plasma weapons.

Beam Cannon - Upgrades the cannon. How important this is depends on
how many soldiers are using cannons.

Plasma Lance - Upgrades the sniper rifle. If using the reaper-sniper
strategy this is a key technology. The plasma lance provides
excellent long range support.

Storm Gun - Upgrades the shotgun of the ranger. This weapon enhances
the ranger role of being a hard hitting unit. How important this is
depends a lot on how a player uses rangers. Rangers that do mainly
scouting will not benefit from the weapon upgrade as much.

Advent Data Pad Decryption - Provides intelligence. Unless there is a
dramatic need for intelligence or a breakthrough or inspiration
reduces the time for research to only one or two days this technology
can be put on the back burner.

Alien Data Cache Decryption - Provides intelligence. This technology
can be ignored unless the need for intelligence is very great.

Facility Lead - If the Avatar countdown has started this technology
should be researched immediately if no facilities are already
accessible. Otherwise, it can be held in reserve until needed.

Experimental Weapons - Makes the hunter's ax, bolt caster, frost bomb
and shadow keeper available in the proving ground. The frost bomb is
the most useful of these weapons as it can give more time to deal
with the most dangerous enemies. The shadow keeper's main ability is
not so useful since snipers are seldom in the front lines. The
shadow keeper is best suited to a gunslinger style sniper. The
hunter's ax's throwing ability since it is a one-shot per mission is
less useful. The bolt caster has a stun ability but its rate of fire
can become an issue on some missions, especially ones with the lost.
This technology is worth it for the frost bomb.

Assassin Weapons - Provides the arashi and katana. The arashi is an excellent close range weapon with superior upgrades. The katana ignore up to five armor, dodge and defense making it a very dangerous weapon. The assassin weapons are well suited to the ranger or any class that deals in close combat.

Hunter Weapons - Provides the Darklance and Darkclaw, both excellent weapons for a sniper. The Darklance has superior upgrades and the Darkclaw ignores up to five armor making it a very effective pistol.

Warlock Weapons - Provides the disruptor rifle which has superior upgrades and always critically hits psionic enemies. Several classes can use this weapon making it very versatile.

Shadow Chamber Projects

Blacksite Vial - Acquired at the Blacksite this opens up the forge facility mission. There will be a sectopod on this mission so make sure troops have access to shredding and bluescreen ammo.

Recovered Advent Stasis Suit - Acquired from the Advent forge facility this must be researched as part of the path for the final mission.

Codex Brain - Opens up the Codex Brain Coordinates mission.

Psionic Gate - Needed as part of the main story line. The shadow chamber must be upgraded before this research can be done.

Encrypted Codex Data - Opens up the ability to skulljack a codex in order to encounter an Avatar as part of the main story line.

Avatar Autopsy - Makes the final missions available. This research must be done last.

Autopsies

Important autopsies are in italics. In the standard game autopsies will eventually become instant so these are overall less important than the standard research projects.

Advent Officer Autopsy - Required to build the proving ground. Also makes Advent and spectre autopsies available. This autopsy opens up the autopsies of aliens.

Advent MEC Breakdown - Required for gremlin mark II and bluescreen protocol. This technology becomes more important as stronger mechanical enemies appear.

Advent Turret Breakdown - Makes the defense matrix available. The defense matrix makes Avenger defenses much easier so, if possible, get this done before any Avenger defenses.

Advent Priest Autopsy - Makes the sustaining sphere available.

Advent Purifier Autopsy - Makes reinforced underlay available.

Advent Shieldbearer Autopsy - Makes experimental armor available.

Advent Stun Lancer Autopsy - Makes the ionic versions of the sword, ripjack and ax available. This is an important upgrade of melee weapons.

Advent Trooper Autopsy - Makes battle scanners available. battle scanners are very important when dealing with the Chosen Assassin or assaulting the Chosen Assassin's facility. Chryssalids, although hidden. Can also be dealt with using overwatch.

The Lost Autopsy - Makes the ultrasonic lure available. The ultrasonic lure is not as useful as many other items.

Sectoid Autopsy - Makes the psionic lab available as well as the mind shield. Mind shields can be very useful on units like reapers, Templar and rangers which can often be far from other units.

Faceless Autopsy - Makes the mimic beacon available. The mimic beacon and frost bomb are two of the best defensive items.

Chryssalids Autopsy - Makes hellweave available.

Viper Autopsy - Makes battlefield medicine available in the proving ground, important for the later game.

Muton Autopsy - Makes advanced grenade launchers and plasma grenades available. This is an important upgrade for both items.

Berserker Autopsy - Makes overdrive serum available.

Archon Autopsy - Makes fusion versions of swords, ripjacks and axes available. This autopsy is also required for plasma lance research.

Spectre Autopsy - Makes refraction field available.

Andromedon Autopsy - Makes proximity mines available.

Sectopod Breakdown - Makes the best gremlin, the mark three, available, an important upgrade.

Gatekeeper Autopsy - Makes the alien psi-amp available, an important upgrade.

Viper King Autopsy - Makes the Serpent Suit available. The Serpent Suit is very useful for snipers. It is also good in any missions with vipers.

Berserker Queen Autopsy - Makes the Rage Suit available. The rage suit has a heavy weapon which makes this suit a very good choice. This suit is good for retaliation missions that typically have berserkers in numbers.

Archon King Autopsy - Makes Icarus Armor available. The Icarus Armor is good for snipers for mobility or for front line soldiers when dealing with archons.

Covert Actions

Sabotage - Reduces Avatar Project progress. The Avatar Project can be kept in check for a long time by using covert actions.

Intelligence Collection - Rewards intelligence. intelligence has many uses in the game so this is often a good choice.

Supply Run - Rewards supplies. A good choice if very low in supplies and don't want to spend intelligence in the black market. There are usually better choices.

Tactical Education - Increases combat intelligence of the soldier.

Combat Preparedness - Awards ability points.

Signal Boost - Gain a resistance contact. Makes fewer resistance communications facilities or upgrades necessary. This covert action is a good choice; it aids expansion.

Personnel Extraction - Provides a mission to rescue an XCOM soldier. How important this choice is depends on the soldier that was captured. Rookies are not a good reward for this type of mission but high ranking soldiers, especially reapers, skirmishers and templars should be rescued.

Tech Support - Awards an engineer. Very good choice in the early game but much less important in the later game when no more engineers are needed.

Technical Advances - Makes a breakthrough occur. This choice can be very good depending on the breakthrough.

Teamwork Training - Send soldiers to form a bond.

Helping Hand - Increases income. A very good choice for the early game but not such a good choice in the later part of the game.

New Orders - Awards resistance order. How good this is depends on the resistance order.

Locate Faction - Very important to get these done early. Each provides a faction soldier and adds new resistance orders.

Higher Learning - Awards a scientist. This is the top choice for the early game. The first scientists shorten research times a lot. Every scientist reduces research time but in diminishing amounts.

Recover Loot - Awards random alien loot. This is often not as good as many other choices since the loot to be obtained is unknown.

Counterintelligence - Stops the monthly Chosen activity. This is usually not going to be as important as many of the other choices.

Dark Events

The worst dark events are in highlighted in italics.

1. **Advent Midnight Raids** - Increases cost of recruits by one hundred percent. This event is a minor annoyance at best. The longer the campaign continues the less of an annoyance it is.

2. *Alien Cipher* - All intelligence costs increased by one hundred percent. This dark event should be countered since it impacts expansion and prices at the black market. Routine scanning is also affected.

3. **Advent Rural Checkpoints** - Supplies reduced by fifty percent. The general supply situation dictates how much of a problem this dark event is. If flush with supplies it is not a problem. If income is low it has little impact.

4. **Avatar Minor/ Major Breakthrough** - Only alien cipher or hunt XCOM could take precedence over these dark events. These should always be chosen if the Avatar countdown is active so it can complete before the end of the countdown.

5. **Resistant Informant** - Alien retaliation will happen two weeks earlier. Retaliations can be tough so this can be chosen if nothing else more pressing is available.

6. **Rapid Response** - Guarantees reinforcements on all guerrilla operations missions. This can be terrible if mods with very tough enemies are being used otherwise it can still make guerrilla operations tougher simply because of the timers.

7. **Alien Infiltration** - Faceless are added to all missions for a month. This can bad on timed missions if XCOM loses concealment too early.

8. **Advent Alloy Padding** - All Advent soldiers and MEC units gain additional armor. This can be a bad dark event to get early in a campaign when soldiers lack shredding. In the later parts of a campaign it is not so annoying.

9. **Advent Viper Rounds** - Advent troops get viper rounds. The poison can be a problem. This is not as bad as something like Alien Cipher but not as easily ignored as Advent Rural Checkpoints.

10. *Hunt XCOM* - A UFO hunts for XCOM. If the defense matrix has been built and the soldiers are available for the mission this dark event can be ignored. The mission will eventually happen so not much is gained by countering it when well-prepared. Reapers and snipers

are very good for this mission in cases where line of sight is good.

Resistance Orders

Best orders are highlighted in italics.

Reapers

1. **Lightning Strike** - Units gain plus three mobility for the first two turns while concealed.

2. *Infiltrate* - On timed missions the timer does not start until the squad has lost concealment. This is very handy for uplink sabotage missions.

3. **Popular Support I** - Collected supplies increased by ten percent.

4. **Popular Support II** - Collected supplies increased by fifteen percent.

5. **Recruiting Centers** - New recruits only cost fifteen supplies.

6. *Munitions Experts* - Experimental ammo projects completed instantly. A good choice once in a campaign.

7. **Scavengers** - All resource rewards from scans are doubled.

8. **Live Fire Training** - GTS recruits finish training as sergeants.

9. **Guardian Angels** - Covert operations will not be ambushed. This can be a very good option if very dangerous enemies have been added with mods. When covert options without ambush risk are available this resistance order is not the best choice.

10. **Resistance Rising** - Plus one resistance contact. Saves on expansion of resistance communications. This order is a good choice.

11. **Resistance Rising** - Plus two resistance contacts. Saves on expansion of resistance communications. This is a very good choice.

12. **Volunteer Army** - On every mission there is a chance a resistance soldier will join the squad. It is always handy to have an extra soldier on a mission.

13. **Rapid Collection** - Supply drops are collected instantly. Supply drops don't need to be collected every time; supplies can be allowed to build so scan for them only when more supplies are needed and save

scans for what is most needed.

14. **Between the Eyes** - Any hit on a lost is a headshot kill. Very useful early in a campaign but not quite as useful later. The lost are not that strong.

15. **Ballistics Modeling** - Weapons research increased by fifteen percent. This is a good choice only if doing weapons research.

16. *Heavy Equipment* - Excavation speed increased by fifty percent. Very good in the early part of a campaign.

17. **Resistance Network** - Contact with new regions is made instantly. Good when intelligence is plentiful and expanding into multiple new zones. Only use when ready for a rapid expansion into many areas.

Resistance Orders
Skirmishers

The best resistance orders are in italics.

1. **Vulture** - Enemies drop additional loot items.

2. **Inside Job** - intelligence rewards increased by ten percent

3. **Inside Job II** - intelligence rewards increased by fifteen percent.

4. **Under the Table I** - The black market pays an additional twenty percent for items.

5. **Under the Table II**- The black market pays an additional thirty percent for items.

6. **Quid Pro Quo** - Black market costs reduced by 33 percent.

7. ***Bomb Squad*** - Experimental grenade and heavy weapons projects are completed instantly in the proving ground. Good for once in a campaign.

8. ***Sabotage*** - Remove one block of Avatar Project progress. Excellent for keeping the Avatar Project under control. This is strongest resistance order that affects the strategic part of the game.

9. ***Decoys and Deceptions*** - All knowledge gained by the Chosen is reduced by thirty-three percent.

10. ***Private Channel*** - All mission timers are increased by two turns. Can really make a difference on timed missions.

11. ***Integrated Warfare*** - All PCS effects are increased. This is a very powerful order.

12. ***Weak Points*** - Any shredding does plus one shredding. This becomes more valuable as the campaign progresses and armor becomes more common.

13. ***Inside Knowledge*** - The effects of all weapon mods is increased. This mod, like integrated warfare, is very powerful.

14. **Double Agent** - On every mission there is a chance an advent unit

will join the XCOM squad. It is always handy to have an extra
soldier.

15.   **Impact Modeling** - The speed of all armor research is increased
by fifteen percent. Good if full value can be gained from its use.

16.   **Modular Construction** - Facility construction increased by
twenty-five percent. Good if several facilities are being
constructed otherwise other orders provide more benefit.

17.   **Information War** - Tech defense of enemies or hack targets
reduced by twenty percent. Not enough of an increase to make a big
difference in hacking results.

18.   ***Tactical Analysis*** - Enemy units lose one action point if
discovered on XCOM's turn. This is the strongest resistance order
that affects the tactical side of the game.

Resistance Orders

Templar

The best orders are highlighted in italics.

Noble Cause - Will recovery is twenty percent faster.

Suit Up - All armor and vest projects are completed instantly. Choose this once when War and Wraith armor are available and build the suits desired.

Trial by Fire - Double ability points gained in combat.

Deeper Learning I - Soldier experience gains increased by ten percent.

Deeper Learning II - Soldier experience gains increased by twenty percent.

Mental Fortitude - Battle madness lasts only one turn. Usually killing the enemy unit is just as effective.

Vengeance - The entire squad gains bonuses for two turns after a squadmate dies. It is best to keep soldiers alive so that this is never needed. If this is useful often something is wrong at the tactical level.

Stay With Me - Students more likely to bleed out instead of die when reduced to zero hit points. Soldiers should not be reaching zero hit points often.

Art of War - Ability points gained by promotion increased by twenty-five percent. This is a decent choice to help provide those expensive extra abilities for soldiers.

Bonds of War - Soldier bonds grow twenty-five percent faster.

Tithe - Resource rewards on all missions increased by fifteen percent.

Greater Resolve - Lightly wounded soldiers can be sent into combat.

This order can be a little irritating when it automatically selects some wounded soldiers for missions when there are many healthy ones that are viable choices for the mission. A large pool of experienced soldiers should be a goal in every campaign.

Feedback - Psionic attacks on XCOM soldiers deal damage to the caster. This is the very best of the templar resistance orders. It is very convenient to have this when dealing with codices. One time it is inconvenient is when on a mission to skulljack a codex. If unlucky the codex will use its area attack and be destroyed as a result due to the feedback.

Pursuit of Knowledge - Laboratory facilities boost research by an additional twenty percent. Many other facilities take precedence over the laboratory.

Hidden Reserves I - Provides two additional power on the Avenger. One drawback is that this order can't be changed if the power is needed for active facilities.

Hidden Reserves II - Provides three additional power on the Avenger. This can be good since many facilities can be built using three power. The drawback is the card can't be changed until the extra power is no longer needed.

Machine Learning - Research breakthroughs are twice as likely to happen.

Tactical Play

Weapons

Weapon	Damage	Mod Slots
Assault Rifle	3-5	1
Magnetic Rifle	5-7	2
Plasma Rifle	7-9	2

Disruptor Rifle — 7-9
Superior scope, superior magazine, superior hair trigger, superior stock and guaranteed hits on psonics

Prototype Plasma Rifle — 7-9
Superior scope and superior repeater

Shotgun — 4-6 — 1
Ten percent critical hit chance

Shard Gun — 6-8 — 1
Ten percent critical hit chance

Storm Gun — 8-10 — 2
Ten percent critical hit chance

Arashi — 8-10
Superior laser sight, superior magazine, superior hair trigger, superior stock, ten percent critical hit chance and lower range penalties

Energy Sweeper — 8-10
Superior laser sight, superior hair trigger and ten percent critical hit chance

Cannon — 4-6 — 1
Shreds one armor

Mag Cannon — 6-8 — 2
Shreds two armor

Beam Cannon — 8-10 — 2
Shreds three armor

Energy Cannon — 8-10
Superior stock, superior expanded magazine and shreds three armor

Sniper Rifle — 4-6 — 1
Ten percent critical hit chance

Gauss Rifle   6-8   2
Ten percent critical hit chance

Plasma Lance   8-10   2
Fifteen percent critical hit chance

Darklance   8-10
Superior scope, superior auto reloader, superior hair trigger,
superior stock and requires only one action to fire

Energy AMR   8-10
Superior scope, superior auto reloader and ten percent critical hit
chance

Bolt Caster   6-8
Fifteen percent aim bonus and twenty percent chance to stun

Magnetic Bolt Caster   8-10
Fifteen percent aim bonus and twenty percent chance to stun

Plasma Bolt Caster   10-12
Fifteen percent aim bonus and twenty percent chance to stun

Helix Auto Cannon   4-6   1
Shreds one armor

Helix Rail Cannon   6-8   2
Shreds two armor

Elerium Phase Cannon   8-10   3
Shreds three armor

Pistol   2-3

Mag Pistol   3-4

Beam Pistol   3-6

Dark Claw   4-7
Ignores five armor and five percent critical hit chance

Energy Pistol   3-6

Shadow Keeper   2-3
Fifteen percent critical hit chance, ten percent aim bonus and
grants shadow fall

Shadow Keeper Enhanced   3-4
Fifteen percent critical hit chance, ten percent aim bonus and
grants shadow fall

Shadow Keeper Powered   3-6
Fifteen percent critical hit chance, ten percent aim bonus and grants shadow fall

Sword   3-5
Ten percent critical hit chance

Arc Blade   4-6
Fifteen percent critical hit chance and twenty-five percent stun chance

Fusion Blade   5-7
Twenty percent critical hit chance and chance to set target on fire

Katana   8-9
Never misses and ignores five armor

Advanced Blades   6-8
Ten percent critical hit chance and twenty percent aim bonus

Hunter's Ax   4-6
Ten percent critical hit chance

Ionic Ax   5-7
Fifteen percent critical hit chance and twenty-five percent stun chance

Fusion Ax   6-8
Twenty percent critical hit chance and chance to set targets on fire

Grenade Launcher
Range four and radius one

Advanced Grenade Launcher
Range five and radius two

Psi Amp
No psionic bonus

Advanced Psi Amp
Twenty percent psi bonus

Alien Psi Amp
Forty percent psi bonus

Gremlin
No hacking bonus

Gremlin Mark II
Twenty percent hacking bonus

Gremlin Mark III
Forty percent hacking bonus

Rocket Launcher   4-7
Radius of four and shreds two armor

Flamethrower   4-7
Radius seven in a sixty degree cone

Shredder Gun   6-9
Radius of twelve

Blaster Launcher   7-10
Radius of six and does not require line of sight by firing unit

Hellfire Projector   6-9
Radius of seven in a sixty degree cone

Shredstorm Cannon   8-11
Radius of twelve and shreds four armor

Plasma Blaster   7-10
Radius of twelve and pierces four armor

Vector Rifle   3-4   1

Temnotic Rifle   4-5   2

Shadow Lance   5-6   2

Claymore   3
Radius of one. Damage and radius can be increased with reaper
abilities

Kai-7 Bullpup   3-4   1

Kai-15 Bullpup   5-6   2

Kai-90 Bullpup   6-7   2

Ripjack   4
Plus one critical damage and plus twenty aim

Ionic Ripjack   6
Plus two critical damage and plus twenty aim

Fusion Ripjack   8
Plus three critical damage, plus twenty aim and chance to set
targets on fire

Shard Gauntlets   4-5
Ten percent critical hit chance

Tempest Gauntlets   5-8
Ten percent critical hit chance

Celestial Gauntlets   7-8
Ten percent critical hit chance

Auto Pistol   2-3
Critical damage plus one

Mag Auto Pistol   3-4
Critical damage plus one

Beam Auto Pistol   3-6
Critical damage plus two

Weapon Upgrades

Value are for basic, advanced and superior

1. **Scope** - Increase aim by five, ten or fifteen percent.
2. **Laser Sight** - Increased critical hit Chance by five, ten or fifteen percent.

3. **Auto Loader** - Adds one, two or three free reloads

4. **Repeater** - Gives a five, ten or fifteen percent chance of an instant kill. Repeaters work on all enemies but there is a mod, Can't Execute These Enemies, which changes this.

5. **Stock** - Gives one, two or three points of guaranteed damage on missed shots but guaranteed damage is reduced by armor. Even with armor stocks will still do at least one point of damage.

6. **Expanded Magazine** - Increases magazine size by one, two or three.

Notes on Weapon Upgrades

1. Laser sights can not be combined with scopes

2. Laser sights increase bonus with proximity to target up to ten percent and are most effective on shotguns.

3. Only one upgrade of a given type can be applied to a weapon.

4. Stock damage is reduced by armor to a minimum of one.

5. Upgraded weapons have the same weapon upgrades as the prior weapon.

6. Stock damage does not trigger repeaters.

Armor

Values: Class/Health/Armor/Mobility/Dodge/Utility Slots

Other Abilities

Kevlar	Basic/0/0/0/0/1	None
Spider Suit	Light/4/0/1/20/1	Grapple which does not cost an action.
Wraith Suit	Light/6/0/2/25/1	Grapple which does not cost an action.
Serpent Suit	Light/5/0/1/35/1	Grapple which does not cost an action, Frostbite, Panic Vipers
Serpent Armor	Light/7/0/2/40/1	Grapple which does not cost an action, Frostbite, Panic Vipers
Predator Armor	Medium/4/0/0/0/2	
Warden Armor	Medium/6/1/0/0/2	
Icarus Armor	Medium/7/1/1/0/0	Vault, Icarus Jump, Panic Archons
EXO Suit	Heavy/5/1/0/0/0	Heavy Weapon Slot
War Suit	Heavy/6/2/0/0/1	Heavy Weapon Slot, Shield Wall
RAGE Suit	Heavy/6/1/1/0/1	Heavy Weapons Slot, Rage Strike, Panic Mutons and Berserkers
RAGE Armor	Heavy/7/2/1/0/0	Heavy Weapons Slot, Rage Strike, Panic Mutons and Berserkers
Spark Armor	Spark/0/0/0/0/0	None
Reinforced Frame	Spark/3/1/1/0/0	None
Annodized Chassis	Spark/5/2/2/0/0	None
Resistance	-/0/0/0/0/0	None
Resistance Plated	-/4/0/0/0/0	Utility Slot for Skirmishers and Templars

Utility Items

Vests: Since the game does not have separate slots for vests they are not as useful as they might otherwise be.

Vests

Nanoscale Vest - Adds one hit point

Hazmat Vest - Adds two hit points and grants immunity to fire, poison and acid

Stasis Vest - Adds two hit points and regenerates two hit points per turn up to an eight hit point total

Hellweave - Adds two hit points and sets melee attackers on fire

Plated Vest - Adds two hit points and one armor

Grenades

Grenades: Grenades are very important for success in XCOM missions. They help by removing cover, shredding armor, and applying additional effects on enemy units.

Grenade	Damage/Shredding/Range/Radius Effect
Frag	3-4/1/10/3
Plasma	4-5/2/10/3
EMP	6/0/12/4

Possible shutdowns
EMP grenades only damage mechanized units
Ignore armor

Flashbang 0/0/12/8
Disorients organic units
Remove overwatch
Don't affect other XCOM soldiers
Use on a sectoid removes mind control

Proximity Mine 6/2/12/4

Smoke 0/0/15/4
Defensive bonus

Acid   3-4/2/10/3
Acid burn (Acid burn does not apply to chryssalids and andromedons.

Gas   3-4/1/10/4
Poison

Incendiary   4-5/1/10/3
Burning (XCOM soldiers that hunker down stop burning.)

Frost   0/0/10/2
Frozen

Bombs: Similar to grenades but greater damage and area of effect.

EMP   10/0/12/5
Possible shutdown of mechanical units
Ignore armor

Smoke   0/0/15/6
Defensive bonus

Acid   4-5/4/10/3
Acid burns (Acid burn does not apply to chryssalids and andromedons.)

Gas   4-5/2/10/5
Poison

Incendiary   5-6/2/10/4
Burning

Ammo: Only one ammo allowed per soldier

Tracer Rounds - Ten percent aim bonus

Talon Rounds - Twenty percent critical hit chance and plus one critical hit damage

Venom Rounds - Plus one damage and inflicts poison

AP Rounds - Ignores five armor

Bluescreen Rounds - Plus five damage against mechanical enemies and makes them easier to hack

Dragon Rounds - Plus one damage and inflicts burning. Burning does not apply to robotic enemies but andromedons an gatekeepers are affected regardless of state.

Misc: Other utility items. Most useful items are in italics.

Overdrive Serum - Bonus mobility, mental immunity and less damage for two turns. One use.

Battle Scanners - Reveal units in a radius of 12. Two uses.

Proximity Mines - Placement does not remove concealment but detonation does. Proximity mines do six damage with a radius of four and shred two armor.

Mimic Beacons - Holographic decoy that lasts one turn or until hit points reach zero. One use. The Chosen are not tricked by mimic beacons.

Mind Shields - Immunity to negative mental conditions

Skulljacks - Used only on Advent soldiers or codices and have a seventy percent chance to hit. Skulljacks result in instant kills. Improved skulljacks increase hacking skills by twenty percent.

Sustaining Spheres - Work like sustain. One use.

Ultrasonic Lures - Draws lost to an area within a 12 radius.

Refraction Fields - Provides concealment. One use.

PCS Modules

Basic/Advanced/Superior

First values are without integrated warfare and the final value are with integrated warfare.

1. **PCS: Speed** - Increases mobility
1/2/3   2/3/4

2. **PCS: Conditioning** - Increases health
1/2/3   2/3/4

3. **PCS: Focus** - Increases will
10-15/15-20/20-25   13-20/20-27/27-33

4. **PCS: Agility** - Increases dodge
10-15/15-20/20-25   13-20/20-27/27-33

5. **PCS: Aim** - Increases aim
4-6/7-10/12-16   5-8/9-13/16-21

Enemies

Enemy: Advent

1. **Advent troopers, Advanced Troopers and Elite Troopers** - Use elevation for the aim bonus outflank or use grenades to destroy cover to deal with these enemies. They have grenades so keep XCOM soldiers separated. Threat level for troopers is low.

2. **Advent Officers, Advent Advanced Officers and Advent Elite Officers** - Take them out before troopers before they make one of your operatives easier to hit. They also carry grenades so keep XCOM soldiers separated. Threat level for Advent officers is low.

3. **Advent MECs and Advent Heavy MECs** - These units have armor and heavy weapons. Their heavy weapons don't do that much damage, but they remove cover. Use grenades to remove armor first and then take them out. They don't benefit from cover, so they are not hard to hit. Blue screen rounds are very effective against them but will not be available when first encountered. If lucky the proving ground or a scanned site might provide AP ammunition which is very good against these enemies. In the early game these enemies are a serious threat but as the game progresses their level of threat is lower, especially when sectopods and gatekeepers start to appear.

4. **Advent Turrets, Heavy Turrets and Super Heavy Turrets** - Turrets tend to shoot once and then use overwatch. If a turret is on a building or something destructible a single explosive will take care of it. Turrets often occur in cities or on trains and make easy targets for snipers. Shredding and bluescreen ammunition will take care of them. Turrets are not mobile, so they are not a great threat.

5. **Advent Stun Lancers, Heavy Lancers and Elite Lancers** - These guys hit hard and are a real threat when they first appear. Take them out before other Advent soldiers if they are close to XCOM. The ability of stun lancers to stun opponents can leave XCOM a soldier short. Rangers or templars with bladestorm can provide some protection against charging stun lancers. When the stun lancers first appear they are at least a medium threat if not higher, but they become less dangerous as the campaign progresses.

6. **Advent Shieldbearers and Elite Shield Bearers** - The shield bearers are more irritating than dangerous. They provide extra shields for nearby Advent forces when first encountered. Taking them out first will remove the shields on other Advent forces and is an efficient course of action. Shredding is valuable against Advent Shield bearers.

7. **Sectopods** - Sectopods are very dangerous because they have multiple actions and are heavily armored. They do not benefit from cover so are easy to hit. Use shredding to remove their armor. Spark units and acid grenades are very good for this and the acid grenades will continue to do damage. A psionic with stasis is very good to have when encountering sectopods. If reapers spot them first sharpshooters with bluescreen rounds can take them out at range.

8. **Advent Purifiers, Advanced Purifiers and Elite Purifiers** - The most

dangerous thing purifiers can do is use their incendiary grenades against grouped XCOM forces. These units can explode upon being killed so don't use melee unless the melee unit has an ability that makes it immune to explosions like fortress. In most cases it is desirable to kill the purifiers with gunfire. When in a group with other enemy units the purifier is an excellent first target since there is a possibility of explosion which will damage all enemy units near the purifier. This can be done by putting a unit or two on overwatch and then hitting the purifier with a sharpshooter.

9. **Advent Priests, Advanced Priests and Elite Priests** - The most dangerous characteristics of the priest units is their ability to use mind control and stasis. Mind control can be countered with a mind shield which scouting units should have. Priests have a chance to go into stasis upon reaching zero hit points so poison or dragon rounds are good for a killing blow since the effect will kill the priest after stasis wears off. Solo priests are not a real serious threat but when appearing with multiple psionics they can be dangerous. Stasis temporarily removes a soldier from the battle and mind control can turn friendlies into hostiles which have excellent equipment and abilities. If a sitrep shows psionic activity then prepare with some mind shields and, if possible, some units immune to mind control like spark units. Psionic units that can protect soldiers from mental effects are also very good against priests. Priests are really dangerous only if in large groups of psionic units.

10. **Advent Generals, Advent Generals M2 and Advent Generals M3** - The Advent General is not so dangerous offensively but is immune to many psionic abilities, like insanity and mind control. Since the general is the focus of missions termination is very important to make missions with generals successful.

11. **Codices** - Codices are more irritating than dangerous due their splitting and teleporting when damaged. Blue screen protocol on a plasma weapon can often kill them in one shot. A frost bomb will prevent them from splitting and teleporting but should be saved for more dangerous enemies. Pistol skills like fanfire and faceoff are very good when codices have split and there are many of them. Their psionic bomb attack disables weapons so a good counter is to have some units with melee abilities that don't need to reload to be effective.

12. **Spectres** - Specters are mainly irritating due to their shadow bind ability and high mobility. The best counter is to take out specters at range with bluescreen rounds if possible but if a soldier has been shadow bound, which will happen, then killing the spectre is the best option. Depending on where the spectre is melee units or a skirmisher using justice can be effective in killing a spectre.

Enemy Aliens

1. **Archons** - Archons hit hard in melee but it is their area attack that causes the most problems by forcing XCOM to try to find more cover while also shooting back. Groups of archons can be brought to heel using a frost bomb followed by gunfire. Melee units are also good.

2. **Avatar** - Psionic abilities and regeneration make Avatars dangerous. The best unit to take out avatars is a reaper with the banish ability which with the best magazine and repeater mods make a kill a good bet. In the final mission try to save banish for the last Avatar. Templars with the ability to switch places with an enemy unit can also be handy when dealing with Avatars.

3. **Berserkers** - Berserkers are melee units only so if they can be engaged at range they are not dangerous. What makes berserkers a threat is a strong melee attack combined with high mobility. On retaliation missions berserkers will often pay more attention to civilians giving more time to deal with them.

4. **Chrysallids** - These creatures are dangerous due to poison which continues to do damage until a medical kit is used or the soldier is evacuated and the ability to create more of them from dead humanoids. Their ability to burrow can also prove a problem. If encountered in large numbers with many humanoids around they can become a very serious threat. Retaliation missions with mainly chrysallids and berserkers are some of the most dangerous missions out there. Soldiers carrying medical kits are immune to poison.

5. **Faceless** - The only real threat from faceless is their unexpected appearance. They are easy to deal with despite regeneration.

6. **Mutons** - The muton is a hard hitting unit. They have a grenade so make sure XCOM soldiers are separated. They have an equivalent to bladestorm so don't engage them in melee. A good counter for mutons is the psionic fuse ability which will use the Muton's own grenade to remove its cover and armor. They are a moderate threat when they first appear.

7. **Sectoids** - The sectoid is only really dangerous if in large numbers due to mind control. They are very weak against melee so templars and rangers are a very good counter against them. They appear very early in a campaign before counters to their abilities are available. Sectoids are of little threat in the later parts of a campaign.

8. **Vipers** - Vipers have two abilities that make them threats, poison spit and the ability to pull soldiers for binds. The second is the greater threat as it can activate other enemy pods. Vipers should be a priority target if near friendly units.

9. **Andromedons** - Andromedons in first form are organic and heavily armored. They also have a dangerous acid bomb as well as a melee attack. Deal with the organic stage by first shredding armor. Sparks and grenades are very good for this. After the organic has been killed the suit itself has to be destroyed. Since it is mechanical bluescreen ammunition is very good for this. The suit does not have armor and does not benefit from cover so can easily be destroyed.

10. **Gatekeepers** - Gatekeepers have two forms, one with an open shell which is organic and one with a closed shell which is mechanical. Gatekeepers are closed most of the time and will close after being damaged if not closed so bluescreen ammunition and shredding are the best counters to them. They are priority targets. Gatekeepers have multiple actions so frost bombs are not effective against them. Psionic stasis is good if gatekeepers can not be killed when first encountered.

Other Enemies
Summoning units are given in parentheses.

1. **Psi Zombies** (Sectoid/Gatekeeper) - Get rid of these by killing the summoning unit.

2. **The Lost** - In encounters with the lost units with pistols, like sharpshooters, are very valuable. If available, rangers or templars with bladestorm make excellent forward units. Headshots don't apply to kills made using melee or explosives. Kills using abilities like rapid fire or fanfire also so not result in headshot kills. Although the lost are vulnerable to fire incendiary grenades and bombs still attract them. Environmental explosions and heavy weapons, with the exception of the flame thrower, also attract the lost. Lost tend to appear in unexplored areas.

3. **Spectral Zombies** (Warlock) - These must be dealt with. Don't let them explode next to friendly units. Summoning spectral zombies is what makes the Warlock an irritating enemy. Don't advance too fast when these appear because it may not be possible to deal with them and another group of Advent at the same time. Rangers and templars with bladestorm come in handy against spectral zombies.

4. **Spectral Stun Lancers** (Warlock) - These also must be dealt with. Their melee attack makes them dangerous. Rangers and templars are again useful. In an emergency faceoff is a good ability to have on a sharpshooter when facing the Warlock and spectral zombies or spectral stun lancers.

5. **Shadows** (Spectre) - Get rid of shadows by killing the spectres that create them.

6. **Viper King** - If first encountered at an Advent facility try to take it out at range with a sharpshooter. Multiple actions, a freezing ability and a bind ability make this enemy dangerous. Freezing XCOM units make them unable to contribute in attacking the Viper King. The bind ability could activate more Advent units and it best to face the Viper King alone if possible. If the Viper King has spotted some XCOM units strike first with units that can't be seen like sharpshooters at long range. Also use any free attacking abilities which won't trigger a ruler reaction. Attacks that do additional damage after the attack like dragon rounds, acid grenades and incendiary grenades are very good against the Viper King.

7. **The Berserker Queen** - The Berserker Queen has significant armor and a very strong melee attack that can stun or render unconscious XCOM units. She also has a scream that can cause units to panic. When facing the Berserker Queen keep units spread out. The frost bomb is very good against the Berserker Queen as is a reaper with the best magazine and repeater mods. Again if encountered first at an Advent facility target it at range with a sharpshooter. It is

advisable to have a specialist that can revive units and a psionic
with solace if available.

8. **The Archon King** - This last ruler to appear is the most dangerous.
Its most dangerous ability is devastation which can stun or disorient
XCOM units. What makes it worse than the standard archon ability of
blazing pinions is that it can't be avoided by multiple units. Fire
grenades, acid grenades and ice bombs are all good against the Archon
King. It is best to take out the Archon King at range if possible.
A reaper with the best magazine and repeater mods is very effective
against the Archon King. Do enough damage, and he will retreat just
like other rulers.

9. **Chosen Assassin** - Since the abilities of the Chosen to vary from
campaign to campaign tactics can not always be the same. One item
(or ability) needed to deal with the Chosen Assassin is a battle
scanner. If operating in an area where the assassin is active check
out the assassin's weaknesses and take advantage of them. Hitting
the Chosen Assassin at range is always good, when possible but the
Chosen Assassin likes to close and attack XCOM directly. Use
scanners to locate the Chosen Assassin. Also check out strengths as
they could influence how to deal with the Chosen Assassin.

10. **Chosen Hunter** - Like the Chosen Assassin the Chosen Hunter's
abilities vary from campaign to campaign so check out his weaknesses
before operating in an area where he is active and try to take
advantage of them. The Chosen Hunter likes to stay out at range so
trying to target him at range with a reaper or stealth-ranger spotter
is worthwhile. Also check out strengths which might influence
decisions before battle commences. The Chosen Hunter, like all other
Chosen is immune to psychological impairments.

11. **Chosen Warlock** - This Chosen is the most irritating due to the
routine summoning of spectral zombies or spectral stun lancers.
Soldier that can shoot multiple times like skirmishers, rangers or
grenadiers with the right abilities make encounters with the Chosen
Warlock easier. The Chosen Warlock's psionic abilities also make him
dangerous. Psionics with fortress can help a lot when dealing with
the Warlock. Check out weaknesses before operating in an area where
the Chosen Warlock is active. The Chosen Warlock's strengths also
need to be taken into consideration before setting off for battle.

Missions

General Notes on Missions

There are several factors to be considered when preparing for a mission.

Terrain is important as it has an impact on what soldiers to choose for the mission. Missions in wilderness, for example, are very good for sharpshooters. Areas with explosives favor reapers and grenadiers; missed shots have the possibility of setting off explosives. Areas which have limited line of sight favor rangers and skirmishers.

If the shadow chamber has been built then the enemies and their numbers have an impact on not only soldier choices but how to equip them.

Sitreps also provide useful information that impacts choices for soldiers and how to equip them.

The type of mission is an important factor; some missions are timed which makes a reaper or stealth-based ranger a solid choice for the mission. Untimed missions often can be used to help non-A squad soldiers advance.

Specialists are good choices for missions that involve hacking as are Spark units.

When very important missions like Advent facility missions and Chosen facility assault missions are in the near future then it is best to save the best soldiers for the job at the expense of the current mission. Regarding the Chosen, when actively fighting one on a mission timers are frozen.

Other considerations include the likelihood of success, whether the evacuation zone is fixed or not, and the reward for completing the mission.

Mission adapt in difficulty based how successful XCOM is on missions. The AI also offers missions with rewards most needed by XCOM.

On missions never dash into unknown territory which might activate one or more enemy pods. Also cycle through soldiers taking one action before taking second actions.

Completing objectives breaks concealment. Soldiers behind cover can not be seen unless they move.

Hacking towers or enemies does not break concealment except when the hacked enemy is in the line of sight of other Advent forces.

Overwatch has no penalty when it breaks concealment.

Hunkering down in low cover is better than standing in high cover.

The closer you get to flanking the better the hit chance becomes.

Completing an objective causes the remaining enemy forces to approach XCOM forces.

Overwatch imposes a fifteen percent penalty.

Reinforcements only reposition on arrival.

Evacuations don't require an action so it is possible to dash to an evacuation point and escape.

Picking up a body does not require an action but putting one down does.

XCOM soldiers randomly get ability points by shooting from a height advantage, flanking, getting a kill from concealment, combination kills and leveling up. Points from leveling up depend depend on combat intelligenceligence.

Reload and use overwatch frequently.

Flanked soldiers have yellow shields next to their icons.

Enemies on overwatch display an eyeball next to their icons. Hitting an enemy on overwatch removes the overwatch; this also applies to XCOM soldiers.

Poisoned soldiers spread poison if adjacent to other friendly units.

At higher bond levels soldiers can remove mental effects on bondmates by moving next to them.

Removing daze does not cost an action.

Guerrilla Operations

The goal of guerrilla operations is to counter a dark event. These operations are always timed and come in several varieties.

The first is the recover item mission. A reaper or stealth-based ranger is very handy on this mission which can be completed at range from the item with a spark unit or specialist. The squad begins in concealment so approach the objective getting as close as possible before breaking concealment. The mission is successful if the item is recovered even if not all enemies are destroyed so if the going gets tough evacuate.

Hack workstation missions are similar to recover item missions. Reapers and stealth-based rangers are again very useful for approaching the objective. Spark units and specialists are also effective in this type of mission. Once the hacking is completed the mission is successful. Eliminating the enemy is optional.

Destroy alien relay missions are good missions for reapers and sharpshooters which can destroy the relay at range. Eliminating the enemy is optional. Sometimes terrain may make eliminating the relay at range more difficult.

Protect the device is the toughest type of guerrilla operation, especially in the late game. In the late game a sectopod or gatekeeper will often be right near the objective and start destroying it right away. A strong squad is needed to have a chance of success in this mission. In the late game it may still be worth attempting this mission if the rewards for the other choices are poor or the dark events not worth worrying about. The corpses can still be a good outcome in a failed mission as well as any loot that might have been obtained.

Council Missions

Council Missions come in several varieties and involve either friendly or enemy VIPs. The missions also offer intelligence as a reward for success. In the case of enemy VIPs the intelligence is only awarded if the enemy VIP is taken alive. These missions occur in cities which are good for sharpshooters. Classes with stealth capabilities are helpful but the need for stealth needs to be balanced against the need for speed. Units that can hit hard and grenadiers to destroy cover quickly are very useful in council missions.

The first council mission type is rescue VIP from Advent cell missions. Approach in stealth to get as close the VIP as possible but if the enemy is likely to discover XCOM hit them hard first. Advent can sometimes cluster many units near the objective so try to isolate pods for destruction. Once the VIP is released reinforcements will soon follow so prepare for that before actually releasing the friendly VIP.

The second council mission is extract VIP. One key difference between this mission and rescue VIP is that the squad does not start in stealth. A reaper or stealth-based ranger is really needed for this kind of mission so that the squad can more easily approach the evacuation zone which is fixed. Hard hitting units like grenadiers and sparks are quite handy for this mission type.

The neutralize VIP mission provides supplies and, if the VIP is captured, intelligence. This mission can be approached in a couple of ways. The first is to take a hard hitting squad and capture the VIP after destroying enemy forces. Another way that gains the supplies but not the intelligence if successful, is to send in a lone reaper to assassinate the VIP, easier if the VIP is near a vehicle which can be exploded by the reaper who will maintain concealment. The benefit of the assassination approach is it gives all the rest of XCOM's roster a chance to rest saving them for future missions.
Supply Missions are a good way to acquire supplies, alloys, elerium, and other loot. The missions are not timed. It is often possible to bring a squad of lower ranking soldiers depending on the possible enemies and location. Reaper-sharpshooter teams are quite effective in these types of mission

Supply Missions

The supply raid mission on a disabled convoy missions are the easiest of the supply missions. There are no reinforcements.
Reapers and sharpshooters are very effective in this kind of mission.

The landed UFO missions are a little harder because they do have possible reinforcements if the signal can not be disabled in time.
The signal can either be hacked or destroyed. Sparks can be useful in this kind of mission. The confined spaces inside the UFO make the mission a bit more dangerous than the disabled convoy supply missions.

The last supply mission type involves recovering crates of supplies and comes in two distinct versions, missions with the lost and missions without them. These are the toughest of the supply missions. On missions with the lost snipers are very useful because of their abilities. Lost missions are also easier if melee units are used that have the bladestorm ability. Dragon rounds or incendiary grenades are good against the lost if in large numbers. On missions with the lost even two sharpshooters can be very useful. Advent does not start evacuating crates until concealment is broken. You get every crate if you kill every enemy and Advent stops marking crates if only lost remain.

Retaliation Missions

Retaliation Missions come in a few different types and can be some of the toughest missions in the game. Success depends on saving resistance personnel and eliminating the enemy attacking force. Success increases supplies depending on how many resistance personnel were saved. XCOM does not start in concealment on these missions. Reapers and stealth-based rangers can be at risk in these missions because faceless and chrysalis can hide. A Chosen will appear in the first retaliation mission.

Stop the retaliation missions involve moving next to resistance personnel to save them and eliminating Advent forces. These missions can be very difficult or fairly easy depending on two factors. One is where the resistance personnel are located and the second is the composition of Advent forces. Attacks heavy in both berserkers and chryssalids are the worst since these forces really go after resistance forces quickly. There are no resistance fighters to aid XCOM in this type of mission. Rage Armor and the frost bomb are really handy in later versions of this mission type. Melee units with the bladestorm ability are very good to take on this type of mission.

Haven assaults are overall easier than stop the retaliation missions since the missions have resistance fighters to help XCOM. The mission is composed of two parts. There is a small group of resistance personnel fairly close by and another group farther away. It is necessary to get past the first group as soon as possible. These missions take place in terrain good for sharpshooters making them useful and the large number of melee units that are often in the Advent force make melee units with melee a very good choice. Grenadiers are very useful for helping XCOM move fast by destroying cover of Advent forces and damaging them in groups.

DLC Missions

The alien nest investigation mission is introduced in the Alien Hunters DLC. It is the first encounter with the first ruler, the Viper King. If integrating DLC content this mission is replaced by the rulers appearing near Avatar research facilities. The many neonate vipers on this mission can be killed with a pistol so a sniper with gunslinging skills is very good for this mission. Melee units with bladestorm are very handy for this mission. It would be a good idea to have some shredding and magnetic weapons before taking on this mission. It is also possible to have rulers appear randomly from the very first; this is the toughest way to set up the rulers.

The lost towers investigation mission is part of the Shen's Last Gift DLC. All enemies on this mission are robotic and at the end the squad will have to deal with a sectopod so it would be good to have a lot of shredding and bluescreen rounds on hand before taking on this mission. It would also be preferable to have at least magnetic weapons for this mission. Units with high aim are good picks for this mission as well as units that can move and attack like rangers so that it is easier to get across the rooms on this mission.

The lost and abandoned mission if chosen introduces the Chosen Assassin, a reaper, Dragonova, and a skirmisher, MOX, to the XCOM ranks. The mission also introduces the lost and the purifier Advent units. The mission has three parts. Two XCOM soldiers go with Dragon ova, a reaper, to meet Mox, a skirmisher., who also with two XCOM soldiers for a part of the mission. The last part consists of the first encounter with the Chosen Assassination and an escape from the hordes of lost. A scanner or a soldier with the ability to scan is handy for this mission because the assassin is quite stealthy. At the end of the mission Mox is captured by the Chosen Assassin leading to a mission to rescue Mox. Grenadiers are quite good for this mission as well as units like rangers that can move and fight. Don't let units get isolated by the Chosen Assassin, or they might be captured.

Stealth rescue is a mission to rescue Mox from an Advent prison. In order to maximize chances take a stealthy unit, a reaper or ranger, a soldier very high in hacking skills so the hacking of the prison door might not be noticed. A speedy soldier is also useful to swiftly carry Mox to the evacuation. It is important to maintain stealth for as long as possible otherwise reinforcements might force XCOM to exit without saving Mox. This mission is limited to just three soldiers so it has the potential to be tough. Stealth missions can recur if soldiers are captured by the Chosen.

Ambush is a mission type that occurs as a result of the Chosen to detect XCOM forces on a covert operation. There are two approaches to this type of mission. The choice depends on the soldiers on the mission. Heavy hitting units like grenadiers and rangers can likely handle the forces encountered in an ambush making the destruction of the enemy a good choice. The other option is to run which is a good choice if units that can move very quickly like skirmishers are on the mission. The Advent forces will often get tied up with the lost. It is also a good option for very stealthy units.

One of the early missions in War of the Chosen is a mission to rescue a VIP in an underground area. Once the VIP is activated reinforcements will start to appear. XCOM must hold out until the evacuation becomes available. There will be sectoids on this mission so a good melee unit is a good way to deal with them. Grenadiers are also a good choice for this mission for destroying cover and weak Advent units. Keep the evacuation close by so that the evacuation when it arrives can be used in one turn.

Rescue stranded resistance agents is another mission that happens early in a campaign, usually very early. It is a good chance to get some rookies some combats experience. A good option is to take a sharpshooter for covering fire from high elevation and three rookies. It is important early on to get as many rookies experience as possible. The extra abilities can make the difference in future missions. XCOM must move fast to rescue the operatives in time.

Another mission in an area with lost involves saving a VIP and two soldiers. Advent is also present so bring a squad that can deal with sectoids and Advent soldiers. The map often has good places for sharpshooters which with pistols are also good for the lost. A stealth-based ranger or reaper are also good for this mission. If feeling bold one or two rookies can be taken on this mission. Rescuing the two soldiers can really help XCOM out on this mission.

Assassinations is another type of eliminate VIP mission with a couple of alterations. The mission has a timer that does not start until XCOM lose concealment. The goal of the mission is to kill the enemy general before the general can be evacuated. The timer appears showing where the enemy general will head for evacuation. A good approach is to try to find the general first if possible which will maximize the chance of a successful assassination.

Uplink sabotage is a take on the destroy alien relay mission. It has a short timer that can be extended by destroying nodes to add to the timer. Fast moving units are a must for this mission. Rangers and templars are good choices for this mission. This mission can appear above or below ground so the choice of soldiers should be adapted to the mission location.

The Chosen Avenger defense mission is a must win for XCOM. Since several guns are firing at the Avenger including a very big gun that does a lot of damage time is of the essence on this mission. Ideally the defense matrix will have been built before this mission happens; the mission happens whenever a Chosen has gathered enough intelligence

to find the Avenger. This mission can happen more than once. If guns
on the matrix have line of sight to the various guns they can easily
be destroyed at range. If the Avenger is in a very low-lying area
with little line of sight this mission can be very difficult, even
with the defense matrix. Take a lot of shredding and a lot of healing
on this mission; it will be needed. The reaper is really needed for
this mission. Grenadiers are also very good for damaging enemy units
and destroying cover that Advent can use close to the ship. Use
stealth to get as close to the main enemy gun to destroy its power
supply as possible. Once it is destroyed time will no longer be much
of a problem. Since this mod has many units mods that add units have
the potential to make this mission very difficult.

     Avatar Project facility missions provide a way to set back
Advent progress. There is no hurry to attack these facilities.
Always wait until the timer has almost run out before attacking a
facility. Always try to have at least one story mission or Avatar
facility available for assault so the Avatar Project never finishes.
If attacking facilities with rulers make sure shredding is available.
Frost bombs can also come in handy against some of the rulers. These
missions are not timed so always take the time to set up ambushes
with a high chance of success. In the spirit of these missions
always try to have facility leads on hand so an attack on a facility
can be made in time. If the facility is not in a contacted region
there are no penalties for failure other than fighting the same
enemies again.

     Chosen facility missions add a factor when planning the mission
and that is which Chosen is in the facility. The Chosen Hunter does
not require as much preparation as the other two.. When attacking the
Warlock's facility having mind shields on the units that can do the
most damage to the Warlock is a good idea. When dealing with the
Chosen Assassin make sure to have scanning ability available either
as soldier skills or items. If a reaper has banished and a vector
rifle with the best repeater and magazine then the reaper is a good
choice for the mission. A good way to deal with the Warlock is with
a templar with the ability to switch places with him to bring him in
range of other units that can do a lot of damage. In the final room
take out the units there first before moving forward so that the
Chosen does not activate with multiple units in the room. Destroy
the ability of the Chosen to regenerate as soon as possible before
reinforcements can overwhelm XCOM. When choosing soldiers for this
mission look for abilities that allow multiple shots so that the
mission in the end room can be completed quickly.

Story Missions

The first mission of games without the tutorial missions is the Gatecrasher mission. Depending on the choices made before the start of the game Gatecrasher will be done with either four rookies or one hero unit and three rookies. Four rookies makes the mission a little tougher. Try to get some loot during this mission if possible. Take advantage of higher elevation if available to increase the chances of a successful ambush of the first group of Advent. If grenades are not used then possible loot will not be destroyed. If all soldiers survive, even if wounded, this mission can be considered a success.

The Blacksite is a mission that results in the acquisition of a vial of material. Expect to encounter a Chosen on this mission. A reaper is good for this mission which is not timed. The reaper can be supported by a sniper. A spark unit, if available, is also useful for this mission. It can move very fast when overclocked which is good for the end of the mission. Make sure to have some shredding and healing for this mission.

At some point the Avenger will be brought down and a defense mission where a beacon must be destroyed will result. Preferably the defense matrix will be up before this mission. A reaper backed up by a sniper is good for dealing with the beacon. The reaper is the best scout for this because in shadow the reaper has fifty percent more mobility which will make it easier to get back to the Avenger.The remaining forces will be needed to deal with the assault. If Advent reaches the Avenger ramp and lives the mission is lost and the game is over so XCOM must go all out to win this battle.. Sparks, grenadiers and melee units like rangers and templars all have roles to play in this mission. If the beacon is destroyed but it looks like Advent will reach the Avenger ramp the Avenger can take off leaving soldiers behind. This mission only happens once.

The Advent forge mission results in the acquisition of an Advent stasis suit. The squad will encounter a sectopod on this mission so it is best to be prepared with shredding and bluescreen ammunition. A reaper and sharpshooter should make up two of the members of the squad for this mission. The rest can be made up of a grenadier, specialist and two other soldiers. A templar can be good on this mission making up part of the group of soldiers behind the reaper.

The codex brain coordinates mission leads to the acquisition of the psionic gate. Many chrysalis will be encountered on this mission along with some Advent units and finally a gatekeeper near the psionic gate. A spark unit makes a good scout on this mission since it is immune to poison. After dealing with the Advent units a good way to deal with the chrysalis is to put all units on overwatch except the scout unit and move the scout forward. Another excellent candidate for a scout on this mission is a templar or ranger with the bladestorm ability. Remember to bring along bluescreen ammunition to help deal with the gatekeeper.The spark unit is also good here since it can shred armor. Soldiers that can shoot twice are also good for dealing with the gatekeeper.

After the Avatar autopsy the next mission will be the network tower. Make sure to have enough intelligence on hand to get all the extra abilities for this mission. In most cases only three soldiers will
be able to used on this mission. Sometimes by expending intelligence four will be able to be used. Adapt load out to what enemies that will
be met on the mission which varies. Good choices for this mission are a reaper, a sharpshooter and a grenadier with an acid grenade for shredding and a frost bomb to immobilize dangerous enemies. The reaper's vector rifle should have the best magazine and repeater available for use with the banish ability.

The final mission requires the very best soldiers armed with the very best equipment. The ruler armors can be very handy on this mission since archons, berserkers and vipers will all be encountered on this mission. Use all points available to add any abilities soldiers may need for this mission. Psionics with stasis are good for this mission which is long and often results in encounters with many enemies at once. The reaper's stealth is the best way to avoid unpleasant surprises in the first part of this mission. A sniper equipped with wraith armor is good for this mission. In the first part the sniper can provide long range fire support for the reaper and in the final part of the mission the wraith armor will allow the sniper to get into position quickly. The reaper can spot for the commander's avatar to hit the avatar pod with void rift and then if in range the avatar can be hit again with null lance. Reinforcements come in quickly in the final part of this mission so killing the three avatars as quickly as possible is paramount.

Recommended Mods

<u>Important</u>: If using mods use the alternative mod launcher which is available at https://github.com/X2CommunityCore/xcom2-launcher. It makes checking that dependencies are satisfied very easy. It also makes customizing mods that have such options easy as well.

Comment: These are some of my favorite mods and at this point in time XCOM 2 has more than 6,000 mods so preferences are going to differ a lot between players. Mods that have dependencies are in bold print.

I. Customization Mods

    A. Expanded Call signs and Nicknames

    B. Female Clothing Pack

    C. Female Hair Pack

    D. Immersive Names

    E. Male Hair Pack

    F. More Nations and Names

    G. **New Heads Pack**

    H. **Vest Slot** - Adds a dedicated slot for vests on each soldier. Vests often don't get used without such a slot.

    I. XCOM Patch Tattoos

    J. **US Army Rank Names**

II. Equipment Mods

    A. Additional Ammo Types - Adds several ammo types to the game. Rounds I don't use and disable in the configuration file are shown in italics. Of the rounds I use shredder is the most useful.

        1. Micro Rounds - Allow more rounds in magazines

        2. Shredder Rounds - Shred armor

        3. Scramble Rounds - Reduce enemy hit and critical hit

chances

    4. *Silver Rounds* - Increased damage against the lost

    5. Anti-violet Rounds - Shut down shields and do bonus damage against psionics

    6. *Vampire Rounds* - Heal firing unit based on damage done

    7. *Enervation Rounds* - Reduce damage done by enemy weapons and have a chance to disable weapons

    8. *Explosive Rounds* - Shoot rockets

III. Class Mods

A. **Proficiency Class Pack** - Builds soldier classes around the roles they play in combat. A Proficiency Class Plugin Templar is in the works as of this writing.

    1. Assault Infantry - Takes on the combat role of the ranger.

    2. Field Medic - Takes over the medical role of the specialist

    3. Marine - Takes on the non-melee combat role of grenadiers and rangers

    4. Marksman - Takes on the role of the sharpshooter but has some stealth ability.

    5. Sapper - Takes on the role of the grenadier.

    6. Tech Specialist - Takes on the hacking role of the specialist.

B. **Proficiency Class Plugin Reaper** - Takes away the claymore skills of the reaper in exchange for a pistol and enhanced stealth skills. Moves into and out of stealth a lot more than the reaper included in the game.

C. **Proficiency Class Skirmisher** - The skirmisher becomes stronger by being actively engaged in battle.

D. **Psionics Ex Machina 3.0** - Reworks the psionics class, adds psionic PCS chips, gems for psi-amps and a new resource, meld.

E. **MEC Troopers** - Adds XCOM EU/EW style MEC troopers to XCOM 2

IV. **Enemy Mods** - I prefer enemies that also add new items or research.

A. Advent General Revamp - This general is a bit stronger than the one included in the game. It has a chance to drop a golden Advent pistol which has soul harvest and adds ten to aim and twenty to critical hit chances.

B. Purifier Revamp - The purifiers gain a pistol and several new abilities. The highest rank purifiers can call in purifier reinforcements.

C. **Bio Division 2.0** - This mod also adds new items and research.
    1. New enemies - Bio Captain, Bio Trooper, Bio Assault Trooper, Bio Assault Trooper with Shield, Bio Rocket Trooper, Bio General, Bio MEC, Bio Faceless, Biozerker, Bio Lost, Bio MEC Trooper, Bio Viper and Elite Bio Viper

D. Children of the King 2.0 - Adds four mini-rulers to the game based on the Viper King. New loot and research is also added.

E. More Robots - Adds riot control MECS, advanced repair bits, sectopod hunters and sectopod annihilators

F. Sectoid Abductors - Can kidnap soldiers.

G. Raider Factions

    1. **Raider Faction: Chaos Insurgency**

    2. **Raider Faction: Global Occult Coalition**

    3. **Raider Faction: SCP Foundation Mobile Task Forces**

H. **The MOCX Initiative**

V. **Ally Mods**

A. **Mechatronic Warfare** - Overhauls the Spark Class

B. **Allies Unknown War of the Chosen Edition**

    1. **Allies Unknown Redux Species: Asari**

    2. **Allies Unknown Redux Species: Salarians**

C. **Non-Skirmisher Advent Hybrids**

VI. **Facility Mods**

A. Facilities+ - Adds upgrade slots to several of the facilities aboard Avenger

B. **Gene Mods** - Adds an upgrade to the infirmary that allows XCOM

to genetically modify soldiers. Make sure to get Mitzruti Perk Pack
to get full benefit from this mod.

VII. **Mission Mods**

A. Additional Mission Types Redux

1. Emergency Extraction - This mission comes in three
variants. Extract a reaper affiliated operative, a skirmisher
affiliated operative or a templar affiliated operative. Depending on
the variant a reaper, skirmisher or a templar will join the mission.
Resistance fighters are also on site to provide assistance. Once the
VIP is released reinforcements will start to arrive every turn. XCOM
must hold out for three turns until an evacuation is possible. Some
of these missions also occur with the lost. The evacuation is placed
by the AI.

2. Rescue Haven Survivors - This is a retaliation type mission. It
begins with two resistance fighters and two civilians being controlled
by XCOM. One pod of reinforcements will arrive shortly after mission
start. XCOM must fight its way to the extraction point. There are
additional civilians and resistance fighters present that can also be
rescued by moving inside their circles. Once XCOM evacuates a unit or
kills all Advent forces reinforcements will start arriving every
turn. The evacuation zone is fixed.

3. Neutralize Avatar Project VIP - This works the same way
as a sabotage Avatar facility mission with one exception. The goal is
not to set explosives to destroy the facility but to capture or kill a
VIP at the facility. The evacuation zone is fixed.

4. Escort Operative to Advent Facility - This is a mission
to hack an Advent computer. If hacked by the attached resistance
fighter all enemy units will be stunned. After the objective has been
hacked there is one reinforcement pod that will arrive and a delay
until evacuation is possible. The evacuation is placed by the AI.

B. **Bio Division 2.0**

1. Mixed Bio Avatar Project Facility - Defended by a mix
of all Bio Division units.

2. Bio MEC Facility for Avatar Project - Ninety percent
of the defenders are bio MECS or bio MEC troopers

3. Bio Beast Facility for Avatar Project - Defended mainly
by bio faceless and biozerkers.

C. More Robots

1. Gatecrasher variant mission with two repair bits

2. Soldier Rescue - Adds security mecs and repair bits.

3. VIP Rescue missions with security mecs and repair bits.

4. Supply Create Extraction mission with security MECS and bits.

D. **Rescue Den Mother** - A variant of the first retaliation mission. The only change is that Den mother is bleeding out and needs rescue.

VIII. **Mods That Make the Campaign Longer or Some Part of the Campaign Take Longer**

A. Marathon - Lengthens the campaign

B. Mission Mania - Doubles the missions in a campaign.

C. RW Realistic Non Instantaneous Autopsies

D. Soldier Development - Soldier skills only improve based on what they do in combat.

IX. Mods That Make the Game More Difficult

A. A Better AI

B. A Better Chosen

C. **Alien Side Goals**

D. Delayed Evacuation